DENNIS E. L...

SELLING TIME
How to sell small market radio advertising

TABLE OF CONTENTS

1. KNOW YOUR PRODUCT……...5

2. KNOW YOUR COMPETITION……...19

3. PROSPECTING…………………….23

4. THE DREADED COLD CALL...……...26

5. NEEDS ANALYSIS…………………...32

6. PROPOSAL……………………….45

7. PRESENTATION……………………..49

8. OBJECTIONS…..………………….58

9. AFTER THE SALE……………...…...66

10. GLOSSARY OF TERMS………...…….71

INTRODUCTION

Early on in my sales career, I was seeing a potential client with a co-worker, and before we had a chance to introduce ourselves, the client asked us what kind of business we were in. I was about to tell him what company we worked for and why doing business with us would benefit him, but before I could respond, my co-worker answered, "We're in the ship building business." I'm sure the look I had was one of confusion just like the client. My co-worker went on to explain, "We build relationships, partnerships and friendships." I had never really thought about it before then, but that is exactly what we do as radio advertising account executives.

As an account executive you will build working relationships with business owners, non-profit organizations, civic clubs and members of the community. Your clients will come to rely on you as a partner in their business, helping them grow that business, and along the way you'll make a lot of friends and have a lot of fun.

The sales techniques in this book will take you through the entire sales process, from making the cold call through scheduling the ads. This book was written for small and medium size markets, and is designed to help guide the account execs that wear a lot of hats at his/her station. But, reading this book isn't going to make you a more productive salesperson; you will need to apply what you learn, before your sales will improve.

My hope is that you when you read this book, it will remind you of some things you already know, but often forget to apply. It will teach you a few new things, and it will act as a reference guide to answer future questions.

1. KNOW YOUR PRODUCT

The first step to becoming a successful account exec is to know your product. Nothing will cost you a sale faster than your competition, or worse, your potential client, knowing more about your station than you do. Without product knowledge you can't build trust. The client needs to trust you with his money, and possibly the "live or die' of his business. You shouldn't ask your client to turn the success or failure of his business over to your radio station if you don't know who you are, who you reach, or what he can expect in return for his investment.

Know the "on-air personalities". Way back when I started in radio, the air staff was referred to as "DJ's" or "Jocks", but now they are known as "on-air personalities' or "talent". It doesn't really matter what the jocks are called at your station – know who they are. Take the time to learn the names of the on-air staff and when they are on. Take the time to learn their bios; most of the Jocks that I have met love to talk about themselves so there should be plenty of information available to you. Do this even if they are satellite feed or syndicated programs. Your clients may want to know more about the air staff, so be prepared to answer their questions. You never know when a potential advertiser may also be a fan with a question.

Know your station's format. I realize this sounds very elementary, but you would be surprised at the number of account execs I have met who don't really know the station format. Stations have become more niche-oriented than ever before. The program directors are learning that you can't program for all of the people all of the time; you can only program for all of the people some of the time, or some of the people all of the time, or some of the people some of the time, or something like that. Anyway, back to formats. Without knowing your format, you won't know who your station is

6

reaching. For example if your station plays country music, that is a simple format to recognize; but, is the music hot country, traditional country, country blues, gospel country... each of these formats are different and reach a different listener. So learn your station formats so you can know your listeners.

Know your station's demo. Once you know your format you can determine who that format reaches. You will know your listener's age and sex, and where they live (we'll talk about coverage in a moment). From that you can get more detailed information from the counties, or cities that your station covers. The county profile will show you population of people of your station's demo in your station's coverage area. It will show household income, average time spent in commute, etc. From all this information you will be able to write copy, create promotions, and tie into events that will have interest to your listeners. It will also help you determine what products your advertisers should promote on your station.

Know your station's coverage area. No, just because your station is streaming doesn't mean the coverage area is Planet Earth. I know, you're probably thinking, "But where would I get this information?" You can find this information on the Internet (or at least it was available when I wrote this book) at *www.radio-locator.com.* On this website you will be able to find a coverage map for your station and lots of other technical stuff, like transmitter location and watts. Some account execs like to talk about how many watts their station has, and that's great if your station is a powerhouse. But if your station isn't the biggest kid on the block, remember: when it comes to determining coverage area, there are a lot of other factors to consider, not just watts. Some of the things to consider are whether your station is AM or FM, tower location, frequency, the terrain and more. If, however, your competition is talking about power simply find another advantage of advertising on your station. I will cover this in a little more detail later in the book, so keep reading.

Know your rates. Every radio station has a rate card – even the stations that never use it. I recommend learning your rates so you don't have to look at a rate card when asked about them. Rate will vary from day part to day part; there will be political rates, standard rates and maybe pre-emptable rates. Some stations have a separate rate card for agencies. Know if your rate is based on net or gross, and who should be paying net or gross. Some stations discount rate by volume, some discount rate by longevity of contract, Know what your station allows. Know the difference between your station's 30-second rate and 60-second rate, and if your station runs 10 or 15-second commercials know those rates. It is a little embarrassing, and can be very difficult to correct, when you quote the client 15 second rates and then learn he wants to run 60's. If your station allows paid programming, the rate can become a little complex. Most stations that carry paid programming will have a set rate for half hour or hour long programs, and will only air those programs at times that won't take away from local commercials.

Packages. I have never cared much for packages, a one-size-fits-all approach to advertising. When selling packages, the client needs to be resold when the package has run its course, usually about six weeks. The package usually has a discounted rate; another thing I have never been fond of. And of course, your station is only as good as its next package. Don't get me wrong – every station needs a package occasionally, to entice new clients to try radio, to tie into local events and promotions, or just to stay competitive with the other stations in town. But I suggest that packages be included in the overall advertising campaign, whether that is done quarterly, annually or somewhere in between.

Here is an example.

Let's say, just for fun, you're in the market for a new roof on your house. Then, one day a contractor drives through your neighborhood (let's call him Joe). Joe sees you out mowing your lawn. Joe stops and tells you how great your home would look with a new picket fence, and he could build you one at a great neighborhood *package* discount. You probably would tell Joe that you're busy and you're not interested in a fence. Joe hands you his card, tells you to give him a call if you change your mind and drives away. Amazingly enough, it's just a few minutes later and another contractor comes by and stops to talk to you. This contractor (let's call him Mike) tells you he is working in your neighborhood and a neighbor suggested he talk to you. Mike asks if there is anything about your house that you would like to see improved. You tell him that you need a new roof, so Mike tells you he will work up an estimate and get back to you. The next day Mike comes back with a written *proposal* at a fair price and as an *added value*, Mike is going to build a picket fence at a discounted price. Well, how could you say no to a deal like that – getting a new roof and a picket fence at one low price? Now you're *soooo* happy you tell all your friends about the great contractor you found. Life is good!

As an account executive, you want to be like Mike. You want to find the client's need and fill that need. You also want to get a referral when ever possible 'cause people buy from people they know and trust.

And finally, the words every account exec will hear over and over from any agency they deal with: "added value". As a sales manager, I would allow my staff to offer added value by negotiating dayparts, bonus or discount an overnight schedule, or give the client a website link. I always made sure the account exec showed the client the full value of the "added value", and never offer any, except to close the order. After all it's not *added* value if it's always included in the sale.

Promotions. There are several types of promotions, and oftentimes radio stations don't take full advantage of the moneymaking opportunities promotions offer. Promotions are usually a fun part of the job. Some stations have a promotions director; at other stations the promotions director and general sales manager are one in the same. But either way the account exec is going to be on the front line and the first contact for the client. As a sales manager and promotions director I wanted to see a few constants in every promotion our stations took part in. I wanted the promotions to only last 6 to 8 weeks maximum. I found that any longer than that and interest would wane. Not only would our listeners start to lose interest, but so would the sales staff and the on-air staff. The promotions had to be simple – all promotions needed to be able to be explained by the on-air staff in just a few seconds. All promotions needed to have listener participation. The more involved the listeners could be, the more excitement would be generated for the advertisers. And finally, all promotions had to be sellable. When it comes to sponsors, I believe the more the merrier. The most obvious of these types of promotions are station promotions. Station promotions are usually an annual event, and may include anything from non-profit community fundraisers to simple on air contests. Selling sponsorships to a food drive, toy drive or coat drive is pretty straight-forward and is easily promoted on air, and through other media if your station is so inclined. Over the years I have seen several non-profit organizations actually plan their budgets based on annual contributions from local radio stations. Non-profit fundraisers are a win-win-win. The station makes money from sponsors, the organization benefits from the contributions, and the advertisers sell more products and add to their positive image by helping the community.

Promotions such as concert tickets, dinner certificates, movie passes, etc. can be *sponsored* on-air contests. Or, if the concert or event is a big enough draw, sell point-of-entry sponsorships to local merchants. Point-of-entry locations are a great way to increase foot traffic for a local retailer. These promotions can be a *package* to introduce new clients to radio.

Client promotions are often overlooked. I have seen several clients over the years tell me they had no advertising budget, or didn't advertise on radio. But when asked, they would oftentimes have promotional budgets. Many times manufactures will provide promotional co-op dollars for specific events. For example, I worked with a clothing retailer that had co-op money available for a fashion show, but didn't have money available for radio, so my station put on a fashion show. I sold the show to another client in a cross promotion. I will get to cross promotions in just a moment. There are almost as many opportunities for client promotions as there are clients. When you do your Needs Analysis, always try to learn if the client has promotional dollars, and learn if the client has anniversary sales or specific holiday sales that a promotion can be built around. Don't overlook the promotional monies available through co-op. And oftentimes client promotions will generate as much exposure for the station as a station promotion will.

Cross promotions are another way for a station to generate revenue where otherwise there would be no sales. Shopping centers and strip malls often have little or no advertising budget and the retailers in the center also have very limited funds. But by creating a promotion at the center that each business contributes a small amount to, you suddenly have a budget for a promotion. Another great way to do cross promotions is to sell booth space at an already existing promotion. I had a shopping center as a client that had a very limited budget, but the center had a lot of excess parking. The center would spend the budget it had for a promotion held in its parking lot. The merchants would provide prizes and sometimes ad dollars. Over the years, my station had classic car shows sponsored by body shops, parts stores and insurance companies; we had Halloween costume contests sponsor by costume shops, and toy stores; we had bicycle safety classes for kids, and several other promotions. The idea was to provide advertisers from outside the center (non-competing with center businesses of course) with the foot traffic the center and the promotion created. These types of promotions are great exposure for the station – they build great relationships with businesses from the center and beyond, and they generate revenue. These type of cross promotions aren't limited to just shopping centers. Any business can cross promote with a complimentary business. For example: used car dealers and paint shops, insurance companies, auto parts stores; work wear stores with truck dealers and tool shops; travel agencies with airlines or hotel chains. Use your imagination, be creative and I'm sure you will come up with some great cross- promotion ideas.

Another source of promotional revenue is to tie in with local events. Oftentimes, when selling advertising to local events such as city or county fairs or local concerts, space for resale can be negotiated. Booth space at a concert or fair is valuable real estate. The foot traffic is usually a very high count, and when advertisers can combine advertising to the event it is quite successful. When reselling the booth space always include airtime in the price. This way you can charge more for the space than the fair would, (they don't want to compete with you) and you can show the client the power of radio. The great thing about tying in with an existing event is that the heavy lifting is already done. The foot traffic will already be there and the event is paying for the promotion. In most markets there are far more events each year than a station can attend, so choose events that best fit your station's format. If there are still too many, narrow the choice down by the body count or by which will produce the most revenue. The summer months are usually filled with events, but remember to service your regular advertising accounts as well. The best three things you can do for advertisers are service, service, and service.

2. KNOW YOUR COMPETITION

Let's take a look at who your competition really is. The first and most obvious of course are the other radio stations in your area. Also other obvious competitors would be the local newspaper, direct mail, billboards, buses, phone books, cable TV, the internet, the little signs on shopping carts, the coupons on the back of your grocery receipt...the list goes on. But the not-so-obvious competition might be that trip to Mexico the storeowner wants to take, or perhaps he wants to enlarge his store, or relocate. The idea is that most business owners look at advertising as an expense and not an investment, so when you ask him to purchase advertising the first thing he thinks is, "Where will I cut back to pay for it?" Keeping that in mind, we will first look at how to deal with your obvious competition, and will get to the not-so-obvious later (the suspense will keep you reading).

In regard to the other radio stations, you should learn the same information about them that you learn about your own station. Earlier I told you one of the fastest ways to lose a sale was to have your competition know more about your station than you do. Well, that also works in reverse. Know more about your competitor's station than its account execs know, and you will have a better chance of earning your client's trust.

Take the time to learn as much about each competitor as possible. Know the other radio stations' rates, what annual promotions they do, what local events they tie into, what packages they offer, their coverage areas, demographics, etc. You can usually get all this information by simply asking your clients what the other stations are offering. Get a copy of their media kit, look at their phone book ads and, of course, listen to their stations. I *know* you probably don't like the music and the DJ's aren't as funny and clever as yours, but man up, it's what you have to do to be All Knowing. Know how many phone books are in your coverage area; there are usually several. Also, learn how many of each book is delivered. This can be done with a phone call. You should know the cost per column inch of your local newspaper and *that* circulation. Learn cost and number of mailings for all the local direct mail companies…well you get the idea.

Once you have learned what the competition is promoting out on the street, it will be much easier for you to overcome any packages or proposals your clients may be considering. Again, knowledge is key – you must find out where and why your clients are currently advertising.

Unfortunately, over the years radio has shot itself in the foot with it's rating system. Radio stations are often asked to show their quarter hour share (the number of listeners during any quarter hour) or their ranking, while newspaper only has to show how many papers they print, direct mail shows how many homes they mail to, and cable TV shows how many subscribers they have.

Radio reaches nearly every house with its signal; ***99% of the population has a radio in their home or car.*** Use this information when overcoming a client's objection to your station. The first step to any sale is to sell the client on the idea that his business needs to advertise (sometimes this can be very difficult), next he needs to be convinced to use radio, then sell the client on the idea of using your station, and finally, sell the client on your proposal. I was once told, "Whenever I made a presentation to a client a sale would be made. Either I would sell the client on why he should be using my radio station, or he would sell me on why he shouldn't be." When making a presentation, be the better salesperson. And you do that by knowing the competition so you can overcome the objections.

3. PROSPECTING

Most sales people believe that the sales process begins with the cold call. Well, that's not true. The sales process begins with *prospecting* for a cold call. In the previous pages I talked about knowing your competition, reading the paper, listening to other radio stations and so on. During that process you should be prospecting. While reading the newspaper look at the ads, who is advertising? Those businesses are great leads. But even better are the *competitors* of those businesses. Thumb through the phone books; when a business is in all of the local books, they are a great lead, but when a business is in one but not another they need help to compete. The same holds true with all forms of media: direct mail, buses, billboards, the signs on the fence at the local ball field… all advertisers are great leads but so are the non-advertising competitors of those businesses. Listening to the other radio stations in your market is a great source to prospect because the first two steps of the sales process have been done for you. The advertisers on other radio stations have already been convinced of the value of advertising and they are at least convinced to try radio – all you have to do is find their need, and convince them to let you fill that need.

Once you've decided which business you are going to cold call, it's time to start preparing for that cold call. The Internet is a wonderful thing and most businesses have a website, so visiting that site can save hours of prep time. Gather as much information about the business as possible: what products the business carries or what services they provide, and what area they serve. Then check out their competitors' websites and make some comparisons to price, quality of products, area serviced, length of time in business, etc. Look for that businesses' ad in the phone books, watch for their ads on buses and billboards. If possible, even take a trip through their store. Sometimes that isn't possible with service clients. All of this preparation will help when you get to the Needs Analysis with the business owner.

After you have been working as an account exec for a short time, you will realize that you never listen to the radio the same way as you did before. You don't read the paper the same – you may even find yourself actually reading the junk mail you receive. Strange as it may seem, you will find yourself critiquing TV and radio commercials. You'll catch yourself writing down the names of stores while you're out shopping with your family. And in some extreme cases your significant other may give you *that look* when you start asking waitresses or cashiers, "Who handles the advertising for your company?" And why do you begin to act in this strange manner? *It's because everything is a lead.*

4. THE DREADED COLD CALL

The cold call is the most difficult step in the sales process. I have seen grown men breakdown and cry like a baby 'cause they had to make a cold call. I have seen seasoned account executives try to create an account list with so many business names on it that they thought they would never have to make a cold call. They believed if they had a list with enough names on it, someone would always be calling them. Why is it so difficult? I don't think I have ever seen a study done on cold calls, but I believe it has to do with not liking rejection. I know as sales people we deal with rejection everyday and not just from cold calls. We deal with rejection from long time advertisers as well. I also know that most of us have made a cold call and found the client to be excited that we were there to tell them about radio advertising. So why do we hate cold calls? Heck, I don't know; I just know they have to be done.

Some account executives like to make their cold calls in person, some like to use the phone and even others like to use e-mail. Of the three I like e-mail the least. First, it is too easy to hit the delete button – that is if it doesn't end up in a Spam folder to begin with. Making a phone call is better, but you still can't see what is going on at the store. You may be on the phone with the decision maker when a customer walks out. The decision maker now thinks because he was on the phone with you he missed a sale. In my opinion, an in-person visit is best. I realize sometimes the client is too far away, and yes, e-mail and phone are much faster, but I suggest you reach for quality over quantity.

What do we want to accomplish with a cold call? We already know a lot about the business from our prospecting. The two things we want to accomplish with a cold call are 1) find out who the decision maker is, and 2) set an appointment with that decision maker. That sounds simple doesn't it? But it isn't as easy as it sounds. First, there is almost always a gatekeeper whose sole purpose in life is to prevent you from getting to the decision maker. The gatekeeper is usually a front office person, but occasionally the gatekeeper will have a title like executive assistant or marketing assistant. Some account execs try to get past gatekeepers by winning them over with gifts from the station. Gifts like note pads, ink pens, calendars, or coffee mugs. Some will even go to the extreme as to bring them concert tickets or dinner certificates. Other account execs will try to side step the gatekeepers with trickery and deceit. I always liked the direct approach. I would first ask the gatekeeper if they were involved in the decision making process for advertising purchases. If the answer given were yes, I would try to set an appointment with the gatekeeper and decision maker at the same time. If the answer given were no, I would try to set an appointment with the gatekeeper and the decision maker at the same time. What, you ask. In most small businesses the decision maker is going to rely on input from the gatekeeper, so it becomes crucial for the gatekeeper to be as informed about your product as the decision maker. Oftentimes you will be misled by the gatekeeper and they will tell you *they* are the decision maker. The authority given the gatekeeper is often only the authority to say no, and not the authority to say yes. It is your job to find what authority the gatekeeper has and make sure they are included when necessary. Never – I repeat, never – dismiss the gatekeeper as unimportant; many a decision maker has purchased radio advertising on a particular station because it was the station the gatekeeper listened to most. On the other hand, if you can convince the gatekeeper to be an advocate for your station it will be a big plus, and not just because it helps with the initial sale, but because the gatekeeper is often the person the decision maker relies on to track the results of the advertising.

Sometimes you will call a business or walk into a store and ask who the decision maker is, and find you are already talking to him. Your first instinct might be to immediately start asking questions about the advertising and promotions. *Wrong*. The same process still holds true. Ask for an appointment; often the client will be willing to see you right then, other times he will setup a time for you to come back and he may even ask you to give him a call for an appointment.

So, as you can tell the cold call is just to find out who the decision maker is and get an appointment. But it's rarely as easy as it sounds. The most common objection I heard was "I'm not interested in doing any radio advertising." Or, "My budget is already spent, so I won't be doing any additional advertising." Early on in my advertising career I would try to handle the objection by addressing his budget issues, but later realized I don't care about his budget at this point, I just want to get an appointment so he can tell me about his store. I now answer the objection with "I'm not going to try and sell you any advertising. I'm not even sure if our radio station can help your business. But the more I can learn about the local businesses and how they market their products and services, the better I will be able to do my job. So do you have a few minutes sometime soon to tell me a little about your business?" This doesn't always work, nothing ever works all the time. But I have found that I get the appointment more often than not.

5. NEEDS ANALYSIS

You did your prospecting and found a local business that looks like it may have great potential. You made the cold call and learned who the decision maker is, and you were even successful in setting an appointment. Now, the time has come to meet with the decision maker. So what's next? Well, you could just present the latest station package and hope it meets his budget and is designed to meet his current needs, or you could do a Needs Analysis. I prefer the Needs Analysis.

I have included a Needs Analysis that I use when meeting with my clients. You can create your own, but keep the basic information the same. It is not very common for me to actually sit down with the client and start firing off questions. I'm not there to interrogate him, just learn about his business. I usually just ask him to start telling me about his business, and as he starts I let him know I am going to take a few notes. I will ask a question now and again to keep the discussion on track and to get the information I need. Most business owners will answer most of the questions without needing to be asked. I'm certain by now you are asking yourself, "What questions and why do I need them answered?" Well, I'm going to tell you. I will explain the Needs Analysis sheet that is included here line by line, so let's get started.

The first few lines are pretty self-explanatory. I'm old school so I keep a paper trail of all my clients. The Needs Analysis also doubles as a client contact sheet with business name, decision maker's name, business address and phone number. I keep a copy in the client's file. Yes, I keep a paper file. A flash drive is great but I have never lost a file cabinet, accidentally deleted a file, or had the file drawer crash.

Anniversary and special sale dates: These are dates he will certainly want to buy additional advertising and possibly a promotion.

Main products: These are the backbone of his business, and he will most likely advertise the main product more than anything else. You want to research the products features and benefits at a later time.

Co-op: I will cover co-op later; what you want to know is what manufactures of the products he carries, offer co-op. If he doesn't know find out for him. Oftentimes a station is a member of R.A.B. (Radio Advertising Bureau) and can get the information there. Or, get the name and phone numbers of his factory reps and call them to learn of any co-op plans their companies may offer.

Main competition: If you know his main competition you can learn how to get the competitions customers into your client's store. Remember your client's best prospects are his competitor's best customers (and that works in reverse too, so stay on your toes).

USP: the USP is the client's "unique selling proposition". In other words, what does he offer that his competitors can't or won't offer? The USP is the reason his customers shop with him. I'm sure one of the things he will mention is his great customer service, but I have yet to hear a business advertise that they have bad customer service, even if they do. Price is good, selection is good, free delivery, same day service, all these are good. Find your client's USP.

Ad budget: Often the client is reluctant to share this information with you, but if he won't tell you his annual budget ask what he spends per month (including phone books). If he still won't tell you, ask how much advertising he usually does for a sale or special store event. Also ask when he makes the decisions on his annual budget; you will want to give him an annual proposal at that time. The more budget information you can get the better, but you can put together a reasonable proposal without the information if necessary.

Current Advertising: This information will help you a great deal. If you know where he is advertising, the size of the print ads, the length and schedule of his radio commercials, how many phone books his

35

business is in, his direct mail, buses, billboards, etc, then you can get a pretty good idea who he is trying to reach, how much he is spending, and where he can cut back, if needed, to create an ad budget for your station.

Area he draws from: This information will help determine where his competition is located and who they are. It will tell you if your station is covering his current customer base. If you have more than one station, each with different coverage area, this information will be helpful.

Male or female: This information is helpful when writing ad copy and scheduling the commercials. Your station is going to reach a specific audience, but if you know who to direct the commercial to, it will get better results. And if you know when your stations' listenership is more in skewed to the business' customer base, scheduling will also be more effective.

Average age: This information is also a benefit when writing copy and scheduling commercials.

Average purchase per visit: This is the first step in determining the value of a customer.
How often does the customer repeat: This is step two in determining customer value.
How many referrals do you get from each customer: Step three in customer value.
What do you want to accomplish with your advertising: Most of the time you're going to hear "I want new business." That is great, but you need to know how much new business and how fast. I like to compare advertising to putting a pot of water on the stove to boil. If you put the heat on high (run a lot of commercials) it will boil quickly, but if you only put in on medium it will take a lot longer, and if you put it on low it will probably never boil. Unfortunately, several account execs out there will allow the customer to put the stove on low, without letting the customer know that the water will never boil. The result is a customer who believes that radio doesn't work.
How do you track results: The customer will probably tell you he asks his clients where they heard about him, and he may. But his employees probably won't ask. And

even if they do ask, the customer may not know where he heard of the store. I am sure if the next time you went to a McDonald's or Burger King and they asked where you heard their commercials most recently, you would just guess. Also, if he asked the customers on the phone where he heard of the store, he would probably be told the phone book.

Here's an example; a bankruptcy attorney (let's call her Betty) hears a Bob's towing company ad on the radio. Betty doesn't need a tow or a jump-start, and she hasn't locked her keys in the car, so she ignores the ads. She hears these ads everyday for a month on her way to her office and then, it happens – she leaves her lights on at work and her battery is dead and she now needs a jump. Betty remembers hearing about Bob's Towing but doesn't remember the phone number, so she looks up jumpstart guys in the yellow pages and she sees Bob's Towing. She gives Bob a call, and Bob asks Betty how she heard of his company. Betty listens to a couple of different radio stations so she isn't sure on which station she heard Bob's commercials. So Betty just tells him she got his number out of the yellow pages. Bob's yellow pages ads are working great, but his radio commercials don't seem to be doing anything for his company. Don't blame Betty. She doesn't realize that if the commercials don't work Bob will cancel his schedule with your station and you won't make any money. Then you won't be able to pay your bills and before long you will be looking for a bankruptcy attorney in the phone book. But, you won't call Betty; you'll call a different attorney. Why? Because Betty didn't advertise on the radio so you have never heard of her firm. With no calls from her yellow pages ads, Betty is now convinced that advertising is a waste of money so she is only going to use word of mouth. The end result is, you're out of work, the yellow pages rep is out of work, Bob isn't getting any calls from Betty because Betty isn't getting any new clients 'cause word of mouth advertising works too slow so she had to sell her car and is now riding the bus. And it's all because Bob wanted to track results by asking people where they heard of his business. Advertising works in mysterious ways, and there is no perfect way to track results due to so many variables. You might think that if business is better now than last year at this time, when the business wasn't advertising, the advertising is working. That would possibly be true if the competition is the same as last year, the economy is the same as last year, and the overall consumption of the advertised goods is the same.

If, after all that, your client still wants to track results, have him complete a tracking sheet. I included a sample of a tracking sheet that I use. The purpose of the tracking sheet is three parts. The first part is to show the business owner how difficult it is to get his employees to track results. The second part is to show how many of his customers are your listeners. And the third part is a tool for you to use to adjust ad copy or schedule for maximum return.

When I would present a proposal to a client I would occasionally be asked, "Will you guarantee this will work?" My response was, "Absolutely, on one condition." The condition would be that I set the price of the advertised product. The client would always ask what price and I would explain to him I would price it at a dollar. It didn't matter what he was advertising, it was going to be a dollar. The client never agreed with that price of course. But the idea was that if advertising on my station didn't work, no products would be sold for a dollar. If advertising did work and several of the items were sold for a dollar and none were being sold at the advertiser's price, then price of the product was the problem, not my radio station.

For any radio advertising to be successful it has to have four key elements. ***P.O.M.S.***

P. Product The product has to be something the consumers need or want. Trying to sell a half eaten ham sandwich for example would be a bit difficult.

O. Offer The offer made by the advertiser has to be a strong enough offer to motivate the consumer to respond immediately. An all expense paid family trip to Disneyland with each mini van sold might be enough to get a family in the market for a new vehicle to check out that dealer's inventory.

M. Message The commercial has to be informative and clear on the who, what, when where, why and how. I hear way too many commercials, that, although cute or funny, when finished I often ask "what were they trying to sell?" or "So, where can I get one of those?" Make sure the message is clear.

S. Schedule The schedule has to be frequent enough for people to remember. A commercial needs to be placed at a time when people can respond. Restaurants running lunch specials starting an hour or two before noon and running through about 1pm is good. Those same commercials running at 7pm won't have the same effect. The advertised product will have some influence on the schedule. If the product is on sale for a limited time, buy vertical (more commercials over a short period of time). If you're branding a product or company, I recommend buying horizontal (less commercials per day but run more days). Again, it's how fast do you want something to happen.

NEEDS ANALYSIS

BUSINESS _____DATE_____

ADDRESS _____

CONTACT_____

PHONE_____

ANNIVERSARY / SPECIAL SALE DATES ____

ABOUT YOUR BUSINESS:

MAIN PRODUCTS_____

CO-OP_____

MAIN COMP_____

USP(unique selling proposition)_____

AD BUDGET_____

WHERE ADVERTISING_____

ABOUT YOUR CUSTOMERS:

AREA YOU DRAW FROM_____

MALE%_____ FEMALE %_____

AVERAGE AGE_____

AVERAGE PURCHASE PER VISIT_____

HOW OFTEN DO THEY REPEAT_____

HOW MANY REFERRALS PER CUSTOMER___

ABOUT YOUR AD CAMPAIGN:

WHAT DO YOU WANT TO ACCOMPLISH____

HOW DO YOU TRACK RESULTS_____

6. PROPOSAL

The Needs Analysis is complete. You've told the client you will take the information back to the station and have a brainstorming session to come up with a proposal that you are convinced will fill his need.

Now, if your station subscribes to Arbitron or some other rating company, putting the proposal together is a little easier than without numbers. The old rule of thumb was that you wanted a frequency of three. You want your listeners to hear your message over and over again so they hear it, understand it and take action. Research shows that an average consumer needs to hear your ad at least three to four times during the course of a week to process the information they hear and respond to it. I think with as many commercials and print ads a person is exposed to each week, the frequency needed to stand out from the clutter may need to be more than four. NO, this doesn't mean four commercials per week.

The formula using Arbitron or some other rating system's ratings to get a frequency of three is: weekly cume divided by quarter hour share = turnover. 3.29 ("magic number" used for calculating *optimum effective scheduling* to reach a frequency of three) x turnover = OES.

So if your station, KXYZ, has a weekly cume of p 18-35 6A-7p M-F = 18,000 with a quarter hour share of 2000. The station turnover would be nine. So the formula for determining the OES would be 3.29 x 9= 29.61. Thus, if an ad is run thirty times across the sixty-five hours in this day part, it is estimated it will reach each listener an average of three times. Even with this formula there are several additional factors, which will determine the commercials effectiveness.

But, what about the stations that don't subscribe to a ratings system? Go back to your Needs Analysis and determine what the business owner wants to accomplish and how much budget he has to work with. The better the *offer* in the commercial, the lesser number of times the commercials need to run. Also, remember the other parts of an effective radio campaign…the POMS. Some other factors that will have an effect on the commercial's effectiveness are: the competitor's offers (and don't forget about the competition on the net), weather, the economy, and even the indirect competition for the listeners disposable income. So run as many commercials per day and as many days per week as the budget allows. If the budget doesn't allow for enough commercials to run everyday all day then break it down to certain day parts, or run every other day. But stay on the air.

The competition for a listener's disposable income is why a business must continue to advertise. The business must stay on the top of the listener's mind. The listeners' situations change; listeners move into an area, get a new job, lose a job, receive a raise, increase or decrease the household size, or household items wear out. The reasons someone is suddenly in the market for an item is endless. And the purchase is not always timed with the local President's Day sale, or the end of the month clearance sale. The advertisers need to be consistent. How many of us have saved up to buy an item, maybe a new TV, but ended up spending the money on something else, maybe a new washing machine 'cause it broke down unexpectedly? The advertiser needs to be there when the listener wants to make a purchase.

When you put your proposal together, have a couple of options for the advertiser to choose from. Options may include different stations (if you have a group), or maybe a schedule with different day parts. Whatever the difference have two or three prices for the client to choose from.

7. PRESENTATION

You have prepared a proposal for the client. And not just any old "change the 'prepared for' name and use the same proposal every-other client receives" proposal. This is a proposal prepared for this client only. With this client's needs addressed, and within budget, this is a ***great proposal***.

Start with why the client should use radio. There are several reasons why I believe radio is best for my advertisers, and here are a few of those reasons.

Why Radio

1. Reach: more than 96% of the 12+ audiences listen to radio each week. The audience is spread across all demographics (young/old; rich/poor; married/single). In general, radio reaches a huge audience.

2. Radio effectively targets desirable demographic groups: with radio's many formats, radio reaches the listeners the advertiser wants to influence.

3. Radio is uniquely intrusive: It is hard for listeners to avoid hearing the commercials, so radio commercials can break through consumer indifference and create interest.

4. Radio has the lowest production costs of any medium: It is not expensive (especially in comparison to TV) for advertisers to get their messages across.

5. Radio generally has the lowest rates and the most efficient CPMs of the various media. Therefore, advertisers can afford to buy more spots, get more *gross impressions* and build up *frequency* of exposure to their messages. Radio is a good buy to re-enforce messages in other media (radio commercials can remind listeners of ads seen/read on TV and in newspapers). Within a market, there is bound to be some lower-rated radio

stations with rates even the smallest retailer can afford.

6. Radio stations can be combined for *effective reach*: Because rates are generally lower than for TV or the newspaper, an advertiser can buy time on several stations simultaneously, to increase reach.

7. Radio is the most flexible medium. Advertisers can get on the air very quickly.

8. Radio's audience is not as seasonal as that for TV (not so many re-runs on radio). Radio has about the same audience throughout the year.

9. Radio offers advertisers unique creative opportunities -- the so-called "theater of the mind." Radio plays to the imagination of its audience; people supply their own pictures for what is being described.

10. Radio is mobile. Advertisers can reach listeners while they are engaged in just about any activity (including driving in the

car). If you see a person reading the newspaper and ask that person what they are doing, you will probably hear "I'm reading the paper." If you see someone watching TV and ask what they are doing you will probably hear "watching TV." But if you see someone listening to the radio and ask them what they are doing you will hear something like "surfing the net, working in the garage, working in the garden, driving home (or to) work, playing with my kids," you might even hear on a rare occasion "listening to the radio." Radio is everywhere and listened to by almost everyone.

11. Radio has good suburban coverage. This is where metropolitan newspapers are typically weak.

12. Radio is emotional (compared to print). On-air voices can supply inflection, emphasis and emotion; they can make people laugh, hum a jingle, etc.

13. It is easier to measure radio's commercial audiences than the print media's. Print ad rates and CPMs are based on circulation, not on readership. Radio/TV CPMs are based on ratings, which indicate how many people were actually listening/viewing. The argument goes that people are more likely to hear or view an ad on radio/TV than read an ad in a newspaper.

Why Your Station

I can't tell you all the reasons a business should advertise on your station...I don't know anything about your station. But, I am sure it has competitive rates, your coverage area is great, and you have the best DJs, a very creative production department and so on.

Talk to the client about your station's history and what your station does for the community. Tell him about your listeners. Your station's listeners are your advertisers prospects. Talk about the age of your listeners, their income levels, their buying habits, when they commute. Your listeners are what you sell. Let the client know who they are and what they buy. Tell the client a success story about another client.

Do you remember when you did your Needs Analysis with the client and one of the questions you asked was "What is your USP?" Tell the client your station's USP – what does your station offer that no other station can or does offer?

Advertising sales is no different than any other sales in one respect. You must show features and benefits. There are features, benefits and ultimate benefits. Let's say your station covers an entire county (on the east coast that might be the size of an entire state). That is a feature of your station. The county has a population of 300,000 people in your stations demo, another feature. The average income of those people is $100,00.00 per year, another feature. The fact that advertising on your station would influence those listeners to spend money at your client's store, a benefit. When those listeners spend money with the client his bottom line goes up, another benefit. When the client's bottom line is at a certain level the client can retire and spend his day marlin fishing in Mexico... ultimate benefit. People buy for three primary reasons: time, health and love; one or more of these should be the ultimate benefit. I know you're probably thinking what about money, isn't making more money an ultimate benefit? No, money is just a means to acquire love, health or time.

Why Your Proposal

Whenever possible I take a spec spot with me to the client. If I don't have a produced spec spot, I will at least bring a script. I will then give the client a copy of the script (even if he is listening to a spec spot) and a pen. I ask the client to look it over and make any changes he feels is necessary. If he makes a change, he has bought the script. After all he wouldn't make changes to something he was never going to use. Now, show him the proposal and explain how it is going to meet his needs. *Show the value of the proposal.*

The client wants to know how spending his hard earned money with your radio station is going to benefit him. You should identify the need your proposal addresses. Show how using your proposal will help his business grow, or, in some cases, stop the loss. Remember it isn't about price at this point, it's about solving a problem the client faces. If you just talk price (oftentimes that is what a package does) then advertising on your station becomes an expense, and the client will see the benefit to you but not to him. If you show how the proposal solves a problem he is facing, you become a valuable asset. Show the client features of the proposal, benefits of the proposal and the ultimate benefit of the proposal.

8. OBJECTIONS

"This looks good, let me think about it." The stall, yes, we have all had to deal with the stall and several other objections. But, what is the true objection? Finding the true objection is usually the hardest part of handling objections.

Often fear of commitment is the problem, and our job is to eliminate that fear. Sometimes it is just a lack of understanding the radio advertising process. And other times it might be that the client doesn't see the value of the proposal. I am going to cover a few of the more common objections and what I say or do to overcome those objections.

"Let me think about it."
This is usually a stall. If you find out what he needs to think about, it can often be resolved right then.

"Sure that's great, is there something about the proposal you didn't understand that you need to think about? Or is there more information I can get for you?"

"I've tried radio and it doesn't work for my business."
Most of the time his expectations were to high for the schedule he ran. Sometimes the product offer wasn't enough to motivate listeners. And sometimes it's the wrong schedule or too small a schedule to work.

"What radio station did you advertise on? Do you remember the product and offer? What kind of schedule did you run? Because we know every radio station has listeners, some stations have more than others, but every station no matter how small has listeners. So, the question is, why didn't they respond to your ad? There are four parts to a radio campaign, the product, offer, message and schedule. My job as your account executive is to make sure we have all those elements in place so your commercials will do what they are suppose to do. Then radio works great."

"I've already committed my budget for this year."
In a perfect world an advertiser can plan his spending for the year and never have to change anything, but in the real world budgets are adjusted all the time for one reason or another.

"I understand that you have put your budget together for the year, and the budget probably isn't much different than it was last year. But the economy is always changing, the competition is always changing, the consumer's situation is always changing and even the manufacturers products are changing. I've shown you how using our station will help increase sales, So if we can find co-op money from the manufacturer, or possibly downsize your print ads or cut back on color of your print ads, would you be willing to try our station?"

"I can't handle any more business."
This is one I hear often. I understand that certain business is seasonal and reach a peak at certain times of the year. I know that some businesses can't expand or don't want to add more employees. But they still need to advertise to prevent loss to the competition.

" If your business has reached its peak, that is just fantastic. So, now instead of promoting a specific product, you need to keep your name in front of people so they won't start shopping at your competitor's store. Now is a great time to run a schedule thanking your customers for making your business a success. Or, maybe your business could sponsor some public service announcements for your favorite charity. It's always nice to hear a business giving back to the community."

"Does your station have numbers?"
This is often a stall. Most of the advertisers in a small market don't know how to read

the numbers, heck; most of the account execs don't know how to read numbers.

"No, we don't subscribe to Arbitron or any other rating services. They are very expensive and we would have to raise our rates to pay for them. The ratings will show how many listeners a station has for five minutes of any quarter-hour, but it doesn't show how many listeners hear your commercial or respond to it. We know every radio station has listeners, and my job is to make sure that our listeners respond to your ads. I do that by making sure the four elements of your commercial are in place: the product, the offer, the message and the schedule. If we have those four elements in place you will get a good response from your advertising."

"I don't like your station's music, so I never listen."
This is an excuse to not buy, not a legitimate objection.

"We know not everyone listens to our station. And you already shop here so we don't need to reach you. But we have a lot of listeners that don't shop here, because they aren't asked to. People shop where they are asked to shop. If you aren't asking our listeners to shop here and your competition is asking them to shop at his location you're losing a lot of potential sales."

"I have done an in-house survey and not many of our customers listen to your station. So I advertise on a station where my customers will hear the commercials"
Many small business owners will do this type of research to find where they feel is the best place to spend their ad budget.

"I'm surprised any of your customers listen to our station. You aren't advertising on our station so our listeners are shopping somewhere else. You should look at which stations your customers listen to most and cut back on the ad budget there. You should keep a presence on that station, but free up some ad dollars so you can reach our listeners as well."

"I don't advertise; I use word of mouth."
A great deal of long established businesses or small town businesses rely on word of mouth advertising.

'Word of mouth is the best form of advertising. People like to buy from people they know or are recommended to by someone they trust. The downside is that word of mouth is slow. That is why radio works so well. The listeners to a radio station get to know the on-air people. They hear about the DJ's likes and dislikes. The DJs often seem more like a friend than an entertainer, so when the DJ recommends your store or your product, people take that as word of mouth. You can even voice the ads for your store yourself, because that also ads to credibility…people like to buy from someone they know."

"I let the manufacturer do the advertising."
I always like hearing this as an objection.

"If the manufacturer advertises your product that is wonderful. That means half of the advertising job is done for you already. The manufacturer is creating desire for your product, but the manufacturer doesn't normally tell people where to buy. So let the manufacturer tell people what to buy and why; your ads should tell people where to buy and why."

"I only advertise when I'm having a sale."
Unfortunately, there are a lot of businesses out there that follow this plan.

"I think it's important to advertise when you are having a sale. The offer in the ad will certainly help traffic flow. But people don't just buy when there's a sale. Our listeners' situations are constantly changing. People have items that break and need repaired or replaced right away. They get pay raises or new jobs, they move in and out of neighborhoods, families grow or shrink. There are endless reasons why someone would buy an item even when it isn't on sale. If people only made purchases when there is a sale, then stores would be closed except for sales dates or there would be a sale everyday. Either way, they need to advertise."

These are ten of the most common objections you will face as an account exec. If you can learn to overcome these objections either by these methods or by methods of your own, you will be well on your way to a successful account exec.

9. AFTER THE SALE

Once the client accepts the proposal, the first thing you must do is reaffirm the client's expectations. When you were completing the Needs Analysis for the client you asked questions about the value of his customers. Now is when that value becomes important to you.

Each of your client's customers has a value. This is determined by the average sale times the number of repeats, times the number of referrals.

Let me give you an example: If the average customer spends $100.00 each time he shops the store and he returns five times each year, the value of that customer is $100.00 x 5 = $500.00. Now if that customer also refers two other people (they are each worth $500.00 based on the formula) then the first customer is worth $500.00 + $500.00 (1st referral) + $500.00 (2nd referral) making each new customer worth $1500.00 to the advertiser.

If you make this clear to the advertiser, his expectations will be more realistic. So if an advertiser spends $4500.00 per month on your station, his ads need to generate three new customers per month to break even.

Oftentimes an advertiser will assume that if a radio station has thousands of listeners and he is advertising a good offer on that station he will get thousands of customers right away. But that's not the case; it takes time to work (back to frequency), people need to hear a message a minimum of three times. Based on the formula we just talked about if an advertisers spends $4500.00 per month expects 100 new customers and only get twenty, he feels his radio advertising was a bust. But if he is expecting three new customers (the break even point) and he gets

67

twenty, then his radio campaign is a huge success. It's all a matter of managing the advertisers expectations.

Another fear plaguing account execs is the fear of returning to see the client. Account execs way too often sign the deal and then aren't seen or heard from by the client again until renewal time...WRONG! The client needs a little hand holding, especially if this is his first experience with radio, or your station, or you. Get a copy of the produced commercial over to the client. This can easily be done with e-mail. When I first started we recorded on reel-to-reel and customers received a copy on cassette. Give the ad a few days to work then follow up with the client. Is he getting any phone calls, has anyone mentioned the commercial, has his business increased at all? If he isn't seeing any activity, now is the time to deal with it, not two or three months down the road at renewal time. Check the offer of the ad against his competitors offers. And again, don't forget to check the on-line competition. If the product is a luxury item, what is happening with people's buying habits (are they buying non essential items)? Is the non-direct competition eating his lunch? (If your client sells TV's and swimming pool sales are up all over town he may need to make an adjustment). Now is the time for you to look at the POMS and make whatever adjustments are necessary to make his campaign a success. That may mean you need to increase his schedule, move his ads to a different day part, take a look at his offer, or maybe write a better commercial.

If you are the copywriter don't try to be too cute with the ads unless you are going to change them quite often. Cute and funny has a very short shelf life. It's like hearing the same old joke from a friend day after day – it gets old fast. When you write the commercial keep in mind who you are writing for. Are you trying to reach men or women? Are you trying to reach teens, or twenty-five to fifty-four or fifty-five-plus? Production maybe out of your hands, but if you have some input, pair the voice and music with the product and clients image.

One thing to remember is, as an account executive, you're in the ship building business: relation**ships**, partner**ships**, and friend**ships**.

Good luck

10. GLOSSARY OF RADIO TERMS

AC Radio format: Adult Contemporary which features lite Rock and Pop cuts.

Account Executive: A salesperson that sells commercials (air-time) and services clients.

Actuality: An older term for what we now refer to as a "sound bite".

Adjacency: Commercials purchased to air specifically next to (either immediately before or immediately after) a particular feature or programming element.

Aircheck: Recorded copy of a broadcast.

Airwave: The medium for Radio broadcasting.

Analog: A signal with characteristics that is continuous in nature rather than pulsed or discrete nature.

Announcer: One whose job is to reads scripts on Radio.

Arbitron: Name of the company, which provides the Industry-accepted standard of audience measurement for Radio. "Arbitron" can also refer to the actual survey, published 4 times-a-year.

Automated Radio: A radio broadcast that can be automatically controlled by electronic devices and that requires little or no human intervention.

Average Quarter Hour Share: An industry term used in audience measurement. According to Arbitron: "The average number of persons listening to a particular station for at least five minutes during a 15-minute period."

Back Timing: The act of calculating the intro time on a song before the vocal begins and then starting the CD or audio source with that song so that when the preceding audio element (usually something without music under it) ends, the vocal on the song you back timed begins directly at the end of the previous audio.

Bed: A production element, usually instrumental music, but occasionally a continuous sound effect (like wind, for example) that is used as background for a commercial.

Billboard: A short announcement that identifies a sponsor at the beginning and/or end of a program such as before and after road "traffic" or sports broadcast.

Board: A console used to control the audio mix and output of a broadcast.

Board Op: Someone who physically operates the console in a Radio studio.

Book: A slang term that refers to an Arbitron rating period: Fall, winter, Spring or Summer.

Call Letters: The official, legal name of a Radio station. For example: KXYZ-FM

Cart: Primarily used before advent of digital technology, similar to an 8-track cartridge. It is made of analog tape that loops back to the beginning after it plays and is used to store recorded sound.

CHR: A Radio format: Contemporary Hit Radio (formerly Top 40)

Clear Channel Station: 1. A Radio station operating on an exclusive frequency, designed to serve large areas. 2. Referring to any Radio station owned by "Clear Channel Communications", one the largest Radio companies operating in the United States.

Clutter: An excessive number of commercials, which air one right after the other.

Copy Written: Material such as a commercial, a promotional announcement, a public service announcement or any other worded information that will be read by a DJ.

Coverage: a radio stations signal coverage area.

CPM: Cost to reach one thousand listeners.

Crossfade: A technique where the control board operator mixes sound between two sources by fading one down while at the same time raising the volume of the second source. As the second source becomes prominent, the first sources is faded away entirely.

Cume: Abbreviation for cumulative audience. It is the different or unduplicated persons or households listening during a specified period.

Daypart: A portion of a Radio station's broadcast day, usually split up into Morning: 5-10am, Midday: 10-3pm, Afternoon: 3-7pm, Evening: 6-12Midnight and Overnight: Midnight-5am.

Daytimer: A radio station, which is only authorized and licensed to broadcast between sunrise and sunset.

Dead Air: Silence on the radio. During dead air, there is no audible transmission.

Digital Radio: Digital Radio works by transmitting digital audio and data alongside existing AM and FM analog signals, virtually eliminating the static and hiss associated with analog broadcasts.

DJ: Short for disc jockey.

Disc Jockey: A person who plays songs on the Radio and information and other content between them.

Drive Time: Drive Times are the periods between 5-10am (Morning Drive) and 3-7pm (Afternoon Drive) where Radio stations traditionally have their highest listenership.

FM: A method of impressing data onto an alternating-current (AC) wave by varying the instantaneous frequency of the wave.

Frequency: 1. It is an electromagnetic wave frequency between audio and infrared. 2. The number of times a commercials airs.

Gain: Another term for volume.

General Manager: The management employee who has overall responsibility for the running of a Radio station.

Imaging: Imaging is a general term for the type of promos you produce. Imaging is how you position a Radio station within the marketplace. For instance: *"REAL COUNTRY PLAYING TODAY'S STARS AND LEGENDS"*. Imaging defines the station as a product so that the listener knows what he/she will get when tuning in.

Jingle: A produced music element, which is usually produced by professional studio singers.

Liner: An imaging phrase, sentence or sentences that a DJ says over an intro of a record or during a break between songs and spots. Usually, Liners stand by themselves and are meant to communicate concise imaging.

Live Assist: Describes how a DJ creates a Radio show by interacting with a computerized system. The DJ provides live talk, chat, liners, etc. and then activates the computer system, which automatically runs commercials (spots), jingles, promos and songs. When it is time for the DJ to talk again, he/she deactivates the automation and goes live at the appropriate time.

Log: Written record of what transpires in three areas: music, commercial content and transmitting specification. In other words, A music log is a list of the songs played for the day, a commercial log shows which commercials were played and when and an engineering log show the status of a transmitter's specifications during the course of a day.

Music Director: Responsible for interacting with record company reps, auditioning new music, making decisions as to which songs get airplay, how much and when.

NAB: National Association of Broadcasters, a trade group for radio and television license holders.

Package: A specific number of commercials at a specific total price. Usually a discounted rate.

Phone Interface: A phone interface is an electronic device, which allows the signal (audio) from a microphone to be heard by a caller and in turn, takes the caller's audio and directs it into a Radio studio console or recording device or both.

Playlist: The official list of songs a station is playing during any given week.

POT: Short for Potentiometer, a control that increases or decreases the volume sent to a channel on a radio console or audio mixing board.

Production Director: Employee responsible for overseeing the creation and implementation of commercial content, promotional announcements that must be created for broadcast.

Programming: The output or product of a Radio station that is presented either in long form or short form styles. An example of Long form programming is when a station presents a topic in extended length, as Public Radio does. An example of Short form programming is when a station maintains a constant format, such as a style of music where the programming is in effect, small modules strung together

Program Director: Management employee responsible for the creation and maintenance of the product of a radio station with the ultimate goal of attracting a listening audience comprised of a target demographic.

Promo: An announcement, live or pre-recorded, which promotes an upcoming event, promotes the station image, promotes the results of a past event or promotes any other event which benefits the station's image or activities.

Promotion Director: Management employee responsible for creating, planning and carrying out the logistics of both sales and programming oriented promotions

Proposal: A written sales presentation for a proposed schedule

PSA: Acronym for Public Service Announcement.

Rating: An estimate of the size of an audience shown as a percent of a total group of people surveyed

Remote: A broadcast that originates live on location, outside the studio where the broadcast would normally originate.

Sales Manager: The management employee who is responsible for the department, which sells radio commercials and other radio products at a Radio station.

Schedule: The times and dates that a commercial airs.

Share: The number of persons who listened to a station during a given time period, expressed as a percent of all persons who listened to radio during that time period.

Spot: Another name for a radio commercial.

Stop Set: The place where commercials are played during a typical broadcast hour. There may be several scattered throughout a typical 60-minute period. Stop Set length can vary much between local stations and even network programming.

Streaming: the act of turning audio into digital data and transmitting it over the Internet.

Syndicated: a program offered by a network or an independent organization for sale or on a barter basis to several Radio stations.

Traffic: Department responsible for scheduling sponsor 's commercials.

Transmitter: The source or generator of any signal on a transmission medium.

USP: Unique selling proposition. The one thing a business offers that the competition can't or won't offer.

Voice Track: A pre-recorded voice of a Radio personality that is recorded and stored in a computer to be played at a certain time in a pre-programmed sequence of events such as at the beginning of a song, end of a song, etc.

Made in the USA
Lexington, KY
26 January 2013